The Vanishing Ind

Ray Manley: A Portfolio

Text by Clara Lee Tanner

Die Aussterbenden Indianer

Ray Manley: Ein Portrait

Text von Clara Lee Tanner

消えゆくインディアン

レイ・マンリー：ある作品集

文：クララ・リー・ターナー

Happy and Willie Cly, Monument Valley.
Happy und Willie Cly im "Monument Valley" (Denkmal Tal)
ハッピー・クライとウィリー・クライ、モニュメント・バレー

1

Navajoland

Navajoland is a country of eternal beauty, a land of sunshine and calm, a land of spectacular clouds and violent storms, a land of rain and snow, a land of eternal contrasts. It is a land of vast vistas and crowding cliffs, of brilliant reds and powdery whites, of many-hued pastels in piled-up limestone and sandstone layers. It is a land of sparse growth or crowded and majestically tall pines on hill slopes and mountain tops.

In Navajo country warming sunshine can envelop the lonely rider or, threatening but magnificent clouds can send him scurrying for protective cover. The sun can dominate for weeks or it can be covered daily with heavy summer cloud formations. Clouds may come and go, or they may linger and deposit downpours on the thirsty earth. Veritable curtains of water appear here and there along the horizon, summer veils to quickly withdraw, winter rain darkness to linger for long hours. At the end of summer rain violence, compensation comes in a great arching and brilliant rainbow.

NAVAJO LAND

"Navajo Land" ist das Land der unvergänglichen Schönheit, ein Land des Sonnenscheins und der Ruhe, ein Land mit spektakulärer Wolkenbildung und gewaltigen Stürmen, ein Land des Regens und des Schnees; ein Land immerwährender Kontraste.

Es ist das Land mit ungeheuren Aussichten und zusammengedrängten Felsen, mit brillianten Rot- und puderigen Weisstönen, von vielfarbigen Pastellen in aufgetürmten Kalk- und Sandsteinschichten. Es ist ein Land mit spärlichem Wachstum, aber auch mit zusammengedrängten majestätisch hohen Pinienbäumen an Abhängen und auf Bergspitzen.

ナバホの地

ナバホの地は永遠に美しい。そこには太陽と静けさ、壮大な雲と吹き荒れる嵐、雨と雪という永遠の対照がある。そこは広大な展望と押し寄せるような絶壁の地であり、鮮やかな赤、粉のような白、そして石灰岩や砂岩の層が作り出す様々なパステル色に彩られている。草木もまばらな不毛の地かと思えば、丘の斜面や山の頂上には荘厳な松が押し合うようにそびえているのである。

Ashibi Badoni at 78

Hasteen Demsey at 103

In Navajo-favored Monument Valley are representatives of all of the great earth formations which characterize Navajoland; the buttes, mesas — tall, slender pinnacles, — with wide canyons enclosing all. Some Navajos have cherished the beauty of this portion of the colorful land and have lived here for generations; few linger here to this day, some alone but happy in their beloved land. Sandstone formations of this wide Valley reflect the moods of nature, responding to the penetrating light of sunrise and sunset with brilliant reds, or their color dimmed by the intensity of the midday sun of summer, or by the listlessness of winter skies. Multiple moods characterize the play of light and shadow here and elsewhere in this brilliant land.

Despite the high elevation of Navajoland, ranging from a base of about 5,000' to mountain tops of 10,000' or more, and because it is in the great semi-arid Southwest, vegetation varies as much as rock formations. Here will be an expanse of limited or no growth, sometimes but sandy wastes. Seemingly dry canyons can be fed by waters of summer rains to produce quantities of grasses and low growth, or to bring to life and green maturity what seemed to be dead trees. In other areas, spring awakens a myriad of color in limited or more verdant plants, flowering yellows predominating, sometimes extending as far as the eye can see. This not only adds to the beauty of the land but also contributes a vibrancy which wavers only with the disappearance of the blooms. There are stocky growths of piñon, juniper, and cedar, all contributing to Navajo life, some serving for their home-building. These trees may be scattered or they may bunch together in tight growths. In higher elevations are the pine trees which, understandably, suggest holiness to these Indians, with lightning-riven pieces serving for sacred objects.

Another mood of the growth of Navajoland is reflected in the fall turning of colors. Less notice-

Leon Begay

Mary Todechinee at 78

able in smaller plants, it is a veritable shout of goodbye to the verdant greens of summer. Great cottonwoods of Canyon de Chelly become a shower of yellow along their great bending branches, now as earlier a vivid contrast to the red cliff walls against which they are silhoutted.

This Navajoland, which is the largest Indian reservation in the United States, thus breathes of beauty throughout its extent, in the vivid formations of cliff and canyon, in its varied growth, and in the vibrant moods of weather. This is the area which was chosen by many prehistoric people as home, this is the natural beauty which appealed to the later Navajo Indian even before reservation days.

Prehistoric ruins appear in many of the canyons and on open terrain in Navajoland. Among others, Canyons de Chelly and del Muerto were favored by these ancient people; the puebloans built their homes on the sandy floors at the base of cliffs or in the more protected caves up the side walls.

White House Ruins is a fine example of both locations, with ground floor rooms of a multi-storied structure on the canyon floor and the main part of the pueblo in the cave above. What a view up and down the canyon was had by the occupants of this upper structure! Although ladders connected the vari-storied rooms of this and many other prehistoric homes, in some pueblos they were replaced by hand- and footholds cut into the sheer sandstone walls.

Surfaces of walls of these great cliffs appealed to the prehistoric men as desirable spots where they could leave evidences of their occupation of the beautiful canyons. Here they left stories of their hunting exploits, here they drew symbols which must have had religious meaning, here they painted meaningless but time-passing pictures. As suggested, some were painted, others were permanent as they were pecked with a handstone into the hard cliff walls.

Before the disappearance of the puebloans of

Frances Grey Eyes at 90

6

Kee Shelton's Mother at 85

Navajoland and the arrival of the Spaniards, a new people, the Navajos, entered the Southwest, first living north of what is now Santa Fe. Gradually they drifted westward, always showing preference for the attractive canyon lands. One of the most supportive evidences of this movement into the canyons is the abundance of drawings of Navajo style on the red walls and in caves, sometimes close to puebloan pictographs. Also, these men left convincing evidences of the routes they traveled in multitudinous pictographs and petrogylphs along the way such as cornstalks, and, more significantly, a hunchbacked flute player like the one in their sandpaintings.

Once in the de Chelly area, the Navajos spread into this canyon and into adjoining territory. Many of their wall paintings are extremely interesting, with subjects from stars, including star groupings and constellations, to historic subjects such as Spaniards and Mexicans on horseback. There are also the very important "yei" figures which are so significant in the later Navajo sandpaintings. Lines of men on horseback, complete with European dress and some with guns, a variety of indigenous animals, human stick figures different from those of the earlier puebloans, and many other subjects which can be labeled Navajo, testify to the acceptance by these people of this land of beauty as their chosen homeland.

Die Indianer des Südwestens der Vereinigten Staaten sind die direkten Nachkommen der Völker, die hier seit Jahrhunderten gelebt haben.

Die Portraits dieser ursprünglichen Amerikaner reflektieren die Qualitäten und die Gefühle dieser Rasse. Sie erzählen von den Indianern, die keine Angst vor einem Leben mit Kummer und Leid hatten, aber auch mit Freude lebten, den Hass überwanden und mit Liebe überlebten; es verstanden schwer zu arbeiten, aber auch das Leben zu geniessen wussten; die Furcht vor dem Unbekannten überwanden, aber auch am Bestehenden Gefallen fanden.

Und das alles spiegelt sich in ihren Gesichtern wider. Dieses indianische Portrait erzählt die Geschichte der Schönheit ihres Landes. Es reflektiert die Stärke, die sie benötigten um hier in diesem Land zu leben, wo die Schönheit stärker als die Gefahren war. Es zeugt von dem tiefen Stolz der Stämme als solche, aber auch eines jeden einzelnen Indianers.

Die alten Traditionen waren schwer aber gut, sagt das runzelige Antlitz von "Bekay Betsi" aus (Seite 9). Keine Bitterkeit, sondern humorvolle Entschlossenheit in ihrem Gesicht, welches mit tiefen Furchen durchzogen ist, zeugt von ihren Leistungen.

Charakterisierend für manche Kleider der Navajo Frauen sind die mit reichlichen Münzen verzierten Kragen und Vorderseiten der Gewänder, die noch mit wunderschönen "Squash Blossom" Ketten ergänzt werden. ("Squash Blossom" Ketten sind aus Türkis und Silber gearbeitet, wobei die silbernen Ornamente Kürbisblüten darstellen sollen.) Und dann wird das Gewand mit einer bescheidenen Sicherheitsnadel am Hals zusammengehalten!

Native Cottonwood, Canyon de Chelly

アメリカ南西部のインディアンは、何百年も前からこの地に住みついていたアメリカ原住民の直系の子孫である。

彼らの肖像は、民族の特質や心情を映し出している。インディアンは喜びだけでなく、悲しみにも敢然と立ち向かい、憎しみを克服して愛を享受し、楽しむ時は思いきり楽しみ、働く時は骨身を惜しまず働き、そして既知のものを楽しむと同時に未知のものを恐れないことを、これらの肖像は物語っている。

こうした特質や心情は彼らの表情にも如実に表われている。インディアンの肖像は美しい彼らの土地の物語でもある。それは危険であるが、それを補って余りある程美しいこの地で養われた力強さと一人一人の、また部族集団としての強い誇りを表わしている。

「昔の流儀は厳しかったが良かった…」ベケイ・ベッツィの年老いた顔と着古した衣服がそう語りかける（9ページ）。深く刻まれた顔のしわに恨みはなく、決意を秘めた笑顔は試練の後に成就があったことを示している。ナバホの女性の衣服は、首の周りを安全ピンでとめただけの簡素なものである。そして襟元から胸にかけては、いくつもの硬貨をあしらい、美しい青緑色のトウナス花の首飾りをかけている。

Bekay Betsi at 75

Thus the Navajos came to live in this land, thus they came to know the terrain, and the color and moods, the plants and animals of this land. Night skies became a part of their lives and their religion, to be cherished from early years to this day. Earth Mother, Father Sky, steep red canyon walls, the life about them, moulded the Navajo, shaped his beliefs, spurred his imagination, made him all that he is.

And all is reflected in his face. A Navajo portrait is the story of the beauty of his land. It reflects the strength he needed to live in this land whose beauty was stronger than its hazards; it reveals a deep pride of the tribe as a whole and of each Indian. Each face is that of an individual blended into Navajo, each tells of the path followed by the individual in becoming a prideful Navajo.

Portraits of Navajos reflect the qualities and feelings of these people. They tell us that the Navajo was unafraid to live through sorrows as well as joys, to survive hate as well as enjoy love, to work hard as well as to play with vigor, to survive the fear of the unknown as well as to enjoy the known. They reflect a response to darkness

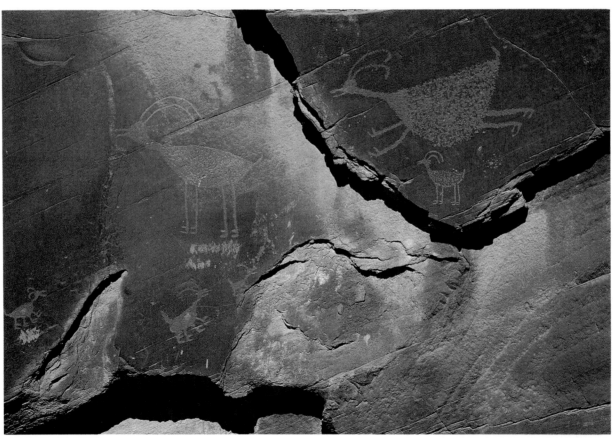

Life Size Petroglyph   *Uralte Felsmalereien in Lebensgrösse*   実物大の岩石彫刻

Denet Yazzie Bekis

and light, to noise and silence, a great void of silence. They tell that the Navajo has known the sorrows of death as well as the pleasures of life.

Perhaps silence is the greatest leveler in the culture of the Navajo Indian, for none can escape it; all who live in this vast land know it well. When grazing sheep, when traveling to the trading post, when attending a ceremony many miles distant from his home, the great, well known, and not unwelcome silence is the companion to this Indian. Perhaps brow furrows were added during this silence as one became part of the

Spider Rock, Canyon de Chelly
Der "Spinnenberg" im Canyon de Chelly (Nord-Arizona)
チェリー峡谷のスパイダー・ロック

Mose Denejolie a 89

endless and lasting beauty of this beloved land, perhaps as one was touched by the unknown. Perhaps all was recorded, to be seen in the depth and distance reflected in deep brown eyes, in deepening shadows in brown-skinned faces. All leave their mark of a "oneness" in life, a oneness and aloneness reflective of the calm and peace bred of vast open lands.

Navajo Indians are soft spoken, slow of speech and motion, dignified of mien; lines in their faces are not belligerent, rather they are deep and soft, they are kindly rather than cutting. One meets with one's fellow men infrequently in Navajo-land, thus it is a quiet pleasure, not a frustration, to see another.

Some lines on these faces are mindful of worry, worry as to whether the little crop along the wash will mature and bear, worry about fresh grazing lands for the small flock, worry about grand-mother who may need a ceremonial "sing" before they return to their main camp. Real needs pressure the mind, deepen the furrows. Limited winter snows and curtailed rains do not promise too much water for coming cultivation, nor do

Joe Tipacanoe at 104

Hosteen Sonnie Bitsie

they guarantee feed for the sheep in the pasture lands. Yes, grandmother is ailing . . . worry succumbs to hope, hope is high that she will remain well until they return to their homeland and a fine medicine man who is known to them.

Laughter is a popular antidote against depression among the Navajos, and laughter lines are abundant at the corners of their eyes. As they sit by the fire in their one-roomed home, the hogan, they laugh about the cold of the day's herding; they laugh as they drive alone in the pick-up truck; they laugh at the miles of walking, of the years gone by; in the comfort of sharing at a large gathering, they laugh at the insignificant nothings which loomed large at some distant and frustrating time. They pass the days, the weeks, the years in joined laughter.

Susie Yazzie, Monument Valley
Susie Yazzie vor ihrem typischen Navajo Winterquartier im "Monument Valley"
ナバホ族のホーガン(住居)とスージー・ヤジー、モニュメント・バレー

Hosteen Bob

A glimpse at a father and son would tell much. The father knew well the harder life of the Navajo Indian a generation ago as can be noted by his more serious and deeper face lines, in the more direct gaze of one who has been tried by the pressures of a difficult life. The son's gaze is a bit away, full of hope, his smiling mouth bespeaks few of life's demands yet the strength and assurance that he can meet them "head-on." Clara John Bee's life has not been as long as her wrinkled face might indicate; rather have the years been long in hardships and deprivations . . . the slight downturn of the left corner of the mouth may be wry verification of this. Yet there are the smile lines coming generously out of the corners of her eyes.

Lucinda Gustine

Tsinijinnie Yazzie at 85

If one has to herd sheep, why not do it in style? (see back cover) These two ladies are happily attending their flocks, favoring two creatures with leashes which are totally un-Navajo. Their smooth skins indicate that laughter dominates their young lives, come what may.

The old ways were hard but good, say the wrinkled face and dress of Bekay Betsi (page 9), no bitterness but determination, with laughter, trials but accomplishments, in her deep facial furrows. Characteristic of many a Navajo lady's dress are the abundant coins down the collar tabs and the front of the dress, all supplemented by a beautiful turquoise squash blossom necklace. Then a modest safety pin holds the garment together at the neck.

Mary Demsey at 84

Alex Belinqache

Pueblo Lands

Hopiland is completely surrounded by the Navajo Reservation, thus is restricted in variety of countryside. Dominant is the feeling of height, for traditionally the Hopis have lived on mesa tops overlooking expansive flat lands below. In those flatlands reside the hope and life of the Hopi Indians, for there they plant their annual crops which are the mainstay of life. Through late historic years many Hopis have moved down below the mesas, first to be closer to their fields, but in time becoming residents of villages which grew in these non-traditional locations.

For centuries the Hopis have been agriculturists, adding a few cattle along the way, and, more recently, some have ventured into a few of the white man's occupations. Although proportionately more Hopis have attended college than any other Southwestern tribe, they remain basically a traditional people. The center of their interests is fertility, fertility of the crops, of man, of all life.

Das Land der Hopi Indianer

Das "Hopi Land" ist vollkommen von dem Navajo Reservat eingeschlossen und ist somit in der Verschiedenheit des Geländes beschränkt. Vorherrschend ist das Gefühl der Höhe, denn traditionell lebten die Hopis auf Bergplateaus, wo sie das weite Flachland unter ihnen überschauen konnten. In diesen Ebenen wohnt die Hoffnung und das Leben der Hopi Indianer, denn dort bauen sie ihre jährliche Ernte an, die die Hauptnahrungsquelle ihres Lebens ist. In spät historischen Jahren sind viele Hopis dann tiefer in das Flachland gezogen, einmal um näher an ihren Feldern zu sein, aber auch zum anderen um Einwohner von Siedlungen zu werden, die sich in diesen nicht traditionellen Gebieten gebildet hatten.

Seit Jahrhunderten waren die Hopis Bauern, die dann aber später auch einige Rinder hielten, und erst seit geraumer Zeit sind einige in die Berufe des weissen Mannes abgewandert. Auch wenn proportionell mehr Hopis als jeder andere südwestliche Indianerstamm das College besucht haben, verbleiben sie trotzdem doch ein traditionelles Volk. Das Zentrum ihres Interesses ist die Fruchtbarkeit, die Fruchtbarkeit der Erde, der Menschen und des ganzen Lebens.

Fannie Nampeyo, Hopi

プエブロの地

ホピ族の土地はナバホ族の指定居住地に完全に囲まれているため、景色の様相は限定されている。ホピ族は伝統的に広大な平地を見下ろす高台に住居を構えたので、高いという印象が支配的である。彼らは眼下の平地に生活の糧となる作物を植えて、自分達の運命と希望を託してきた。しかし近年になり、部族の多くが畑地に近いという理由から平地に移り住みはじめ、次第に部族全体が非伝統的な平地の村落に住み着くようになった。

ホピ族は、何世紀もの間農耕民族であったが、そのうち少数の牛を飼うようになり、最近では、白人が手掛ける種類の仕事に従事する者もいる。他のアメリカ南西部の部族と比較すると、ホピ族には大学進学者が多いが、基本的には未だに伝統を守って暮しを営んでいる。彼らの最大の関心事は豊穣である。それは作物の実りであり、人間の繁殖力であり、すべての生命の豊かさである。

Viets Lollohaftewa, Hopi

This is reflected in their religious organization, with emphasis on the kachina cult, and on native clan organization and priesthoods.

As a small, close society, there are factions at Hopi. Priest leaders command great respect; often these men are intelligent and prideful. Composure and contentment dominate the lives of the artisans; the same peace prevails in the life of the farmer. All of these traits are reflected in the faces of these people, more of certain qualities in some, all in others. Conquering the harsh land in which they live gives a feeling of accomplishment to these fellows, this often reflected in determined lips, in knowing eyes. A far-away gaze in the eyes of the knowledgeable older man tells that he has known drought and near-famine in the past, but the smile wrinkled about his lips tells us that the Hopi custom of storing a year's food supply ahead prevailed over nature's less generous moods.

Thus the nature of Navajoland, Hopiland, and all the pueblo country molded the faces of it's occupants. These were a people who had the time, the courage, and the spirit to respond to a deep beauty, to a harshness balanced by amazing and often hidden resources. Portraits of these Indians reflect a blending of man into lands of great and lasting wonders.

Curley Mustache and son Begay Number 2

Tsinigini Joe

Pueblo Indians of the Southwest are the lineal descendants of people who have been here for hundreds of years. Their ancestors knew lean and fat years, they lived in beautiful lands such as Mesa Verde, they struggled to stay alive, as in bleak and barren Chaco Canyon after drought-depleting years. They had magnificent pueblos with elaborate and ceremonial kivas, as in the heyday of rich Chaco Canyon.

Canyon de Chelly
Uralte Wohnquartiere früherer Generationen im "Canyon de Chelly"
チェリー峡谷

Tapaha Laki at 77

Then came the Spaniards. Life changed drastically in some areas of the puebloans: the old world religion was forced on these people but they kept their own alive by retreating secretly to their ceremonial kivas; new foods were introduced, clothing changed slowly, eventually wiping out weaving; the political order became a combination of Spanish and native. But these Indians continued much of the past, for they lived in their ancient homes (as do the Acomans to this day in their high mesa village which surveys beautiful and colorful country for miles around) or moved to new locations, largely along the Rio Grande River.

Dolyaltic Begay #1 (twin)

Pride of the past, with sometimes its continuation, prevails among these peoples and is often recorded in their faces. The Taos villagers were great traders; success in these ventures is registered in prideful faces and heads held high. Deeply furrowed facial lines also reflect happiness in the pleasure of the continuity of the old ways, particularly in the pueblo styles of architecture at this village; they reflect laughter, too, laughter despite hardships because of the reliving of the happy old ways. At Zuni the past has receded in many material ways, but in religion it lives on. So too is the past relived in the adaptation of prehistoric mosaic to silver and other new materials. Life has not always been easy, as to be noted in weathered faces, yet there are laughter lines at eyes and other evidences of lighter and happier moments in the lives of these puebloans.

Navajo Flock at Slide Rock

Atelth Babbima

The majority of the photographs in this portfolio depict the faces of the Navajo and Pueblo Indians. There are many other "vanishing" Indians in the Southwest that we were unable to photograph. However, we were fortunate enough to "capture" Geronimo III, a Cibeque Apache, at 104. Geronimo III is the grandson of the great Apache warrior, Geronimo.

Die Majorität der Photographien in diesem Portrait stellt die Gesichter der Navajo und Hopi Indianer dar. Es gibt aber noch viele andere vom Aussterben bedrohte Indianer im Südwesten dieses Landes, die wir nicht haben photographieren können.

Immerhin hatten wir aber das Glück, Geronimo III aufzunehmen, einen Cibeque Apachen, mit 104 Jahren. Geronimo III ist der Enkelsohn des berühmten Apachen-Kämpfers Geronimo.

この作品集に掲載された写真のほとんどは、ナバホ族およびブエブロ族のインディアンを写したものである。今回は撮影することができなかったが、この他にもアメリカ南西部には数多くの「消えゆく」インディアンの部族がいる。

シベック・アバッチ族のジェロニモ三世（104才当時）を写真に納めることができたのは好運であった。ジェロニモ三世は、かの偉大なアバッチ族の戦士であったジェロニモの孫にあたる人である。

Geronimo III